CAMP SKIPPY

Becky Roberts

NEWMAN SPRINGS PUBLISHING
320 Broad Street
Red Bank, NJ 07701

First originally published by Newman Springs Publishing 2024

ISBN 979-8-88763-685-6 (Paperback)
ISBN 979-8-88763-686-3 (Digital)

Printed in the United States of America

In memory of my father, Robert Harris.

On January 31, 1922, my dad, Robert Beckley Harris, mentioned to Leona, a girl he rather fancied, that he was thinking about building a log cabin. Her response to hearing that news was, "I'll put lace curtains at the windows, and a white tablecloth."

Dad's response was, "Gee."

That was the first mention of building what was to become my then-seventeen-year-old Dad's summer camp in a little diary he kept from January 21, 1922, to September 18, 1922. The following dates and text were from that diary.

Dad's nickname for my mother was Skippy, and he named the cabin Camp Skippy after her.

Robert Harris and his parents

The family home was on a bluff overlooking the river. At the foot of the bluff was where the cabin was built and is to this day, more than one hundred years later.

Rober Harris with his best friend Bradford. He was Dad's primary helper building the CAMP as Dad called it.

Jan. 21: "Shot a fox down by the further sheep pasture fence (300 ft) with a slug in my shotgun from the back door."

Jan. 26, 1922: Had to stay after school for history. Got over to the village and received a birthday package from Mrs. Bishop. In it was a pair of homemade mittens, a birthday card, and a postal card and two notebooks.
Pretty good, eh.

Jan. 27: "Went to school, carried two qts milk to Chase. Got home. After supper Leona called up and said she and Lina were coming down. They arrived 7 and went home 10-30. I walked up with them."

Jan. 28: "Mother made me a chocolate pie. Going to have it tomorrow."

Jan. 29: "My birthday. Ate the chocolate cake or rather part of it. It was so dam delicious. Got a card from Dorrie (Dad's sister). Says she's coming up next week sometime. Hope so. Don't seem any funnier to be seventeen than it did to be sixteen. We went out and got a Sunday paper for Bill Irish, 2 for Selveh and one for Raymond Mitchell. Got to take a bath now."

Jan. 30: "Went to school. Wrote life of Dow, Calhoun, Webster and Clay make up. Had 40's for not writing them so that brought my rank up considerate."

Jan. 31: "Father said if I shot a fox and sold it I could buy a hound pup in the spring and not unless. So I've got to get another one. Let you know when I shoot it. I must aim carefully and take my time."

Jan. 31: "Went to school and heard there weren't no school Friday. Went off to Leona's and casually mentioned building a log cabin. She claimed she was going to put lace curtains at the windows, white tablecloth etc. 'GEE'"

Feb. 1: "Judgkins paid for milk and I paid the stable rent."

Feb. 2: "'Woodchuck Day.' Some cloudy and raining. Chuck didn't see his shadder. Nothing going much. Read the papers. Did some homework."

Feb. 4, 1922: "Cut down a big white Maple down in the pasture. Used my little ax on it. Pop said I sounded like a woodpecker. William Irish (a neighbor) came up and we went over to the place I had selected this fore noon for my log cabin. I have decided to build it like this now."

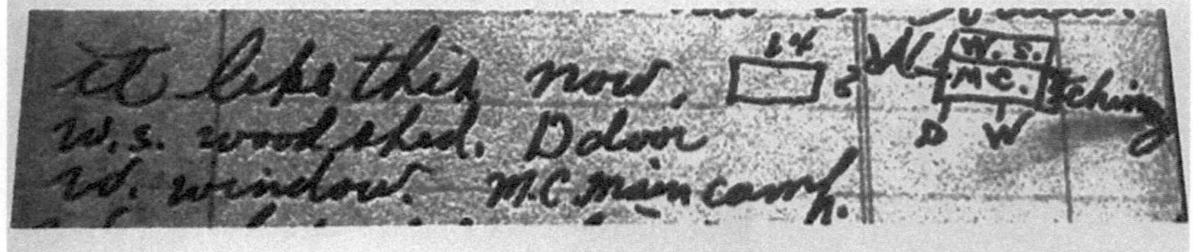

Feb. 5: "Nothing doing much. Went and got Sunday papers for Raymond and us."

Feb. 6: "Snowing out. Been doing so all day. Studying chemistry now. Got home awfully wet and uncomfortable out. Pop reading my magazine now. Got to wait till he gets through."

Feb. 7: "Got my sun watch from Dorrie, Jesse and Barbara. Quite an article. I think Pop's getting reconciled to the idea of my having a fox hound"

Feb. 8: "Read "The Golden Snare" by Curwood in 2 hours."

Feb. 9: "Kicked off the bedclothes and got a bad cold. Nothing much happened."

Feb. 10: "Cold still with me."

Feb. 11: "Mother gathered my jacknife up with some shavings and put it in the stove. By the time I got to it it was plumb spoilt. Didn't go to movies."

Feb. 12: "Had a cold and didn't go after papers."

Feb. 13: "Cold better. Went to school."

Feb. 14: "Bought a globe which same we were supposed to get seen. Paid Lawrence 20 cents."

Feb. 15: "Went to school as usual, snowed 8 inches so far, don't know wether it will blow over or not."

Feb. 16: "Pop gave me 50 cents and I got some school paper and a hot dawg."

Feb. 17: Didn't go to school. Roads drifted. Shoveled some and got to the village in the afternoon to carry the milk to Judgkins and Chase.

Feb. 18: "Took Papa's knife to pieces and put my knife blade in it. So now I have a corking knife. Went to the movies, a lot of people with nuthin on. Cave man stuff, don't you know."

Feb. 19: "Snowing. Went after the papers and got a globe for Agnes. Going to have a sheep killed tomorrow. Sold a hind quarter to French and a front quarter to Chase. I guess I can sell the other front quarter to Staples. Going to eat the other one."

Feb. 21: "Mother got her typewriter (Bought from proceeds of the sheep). We all have wrote on it. No school tomorrow."

Feb. 25: "Helped Paw saw down some trees. Went to the pictures, saw Hoot Gibson in "On the Money Trail" and saw Harry Carey in one of the scenes, standing side o' door, talking to a girl. Bought a queer tree or part of one home. Going to make a table out of it. Bought a spider (frying pan) for camp."

March 18: Saturday went down in the pasture to the site of my cabin and went to the movies in the evening."

March 29: "Good day. Cut some logs for my cabin."

March 30: "I started my log cabin."

March 31: "Snowing out. Nanny had two lambs. Two feet of snow out and still snowing."

April 2: "We went to the village and got a calf of Bill Irish born last Tuesday. One lamb. Didn't get the papers. I got a letter from the game warden. He thought I shot that fox in March instead of January. Made some ice cream. Eggs frozen whole in it."

April 3: "Helped Mom wash. Leona came down in the afternoon."

April 4: "First day of school."

April 5: "School joined the shifters."

April 6: "School."

April 7: "Harry Carey sent me his picture. Autograph on it. Cut my lamb's tail off."

April 8: "Went to Grange in daytime and pictures in evening. Saw Frank Mayo and Dr. Jim (both western movie stars) and an N.W.M.P. (Northwest Mounted Police) picture. Both good."

April 10: "Got the Sunday papers, fixed the pasture fence, burnt ground hemlock and played golf with Pete and Bill Irish, William and Alvin."

April 11: "Sure a working day. Went to school."

April 12: "School."

April 13: "School."

April 14: "One secession (session), shoveled dirt all afternoon."

April 15: "Rainy, didn't do much. Went to the pictures, Hoot Gibson in 'Sure Shot' and a century comedy "Mama's Cowboy.""

April 16: "School."

April 17: "Paid a dollar on my Well's History and sent a dollar for Country Gentleman. Mother went to town and bought me a school suit. $17.50."

April 18: "School."

April 19: "School."

Me with my Dad

April 20: "Ditto"

April 21: "Same."

April 22: "Grange and pictures went to."

April 23: "Sunday papers."

April 24: "School."

April 25: "School."

April 29: "Trimmed apple trees and worked on cabin."

April 30: "Went out after papers and came home through the taper road and got some small trees and May flowers."

May 1: "Went to school and grafted some trees. Got me a pair of overalls."

May 2: "School. Come home early."

May 3: "1/2 session. Worked on my log cabin."

May 4: "School."

May 5: "School."

May 6: "Worked on my log cabin."

May 7: "Went after Sunday papers. Came home in a thunder shower."

May 8: "Sold bushel apples to Pillsbury, going to pay my athletic dues and save 50 cents for a hunting knife. Note: apples $1.00, hunting knife $2.75."

May 9: "School. Set four mice traps and have caught two mice in one of them so far. Got them in a cage out on the table in the porch."

Camp Skippy
Turner, Maine
Cabin built in the early thirties by Robert Harris

May 10: "Went to ball game, Leavitt vs Buckfield at Buckfield. Score 5-1 for us (Leavitt)."

May 11: "School. In the evening, hung a May basket to Ruth Colburn. I ran --------10 miles."

May 12: "School the morning after the night before."

May 13: "Tore the old rabbit pens down in back of my coon house, built a new one and set some strawberry flats out that I got over to Mitchell's in the fore noon. Movies."

May 14: "Started to fence in a little spot for a garden in the pasture but broke my ax handle and had to quit. Jim (Dad's dog) got a chuck in the stone wall. I blocked him in. We planted four rows of strawberries, four rows of beans and eight rows of spuds in the forenoon in the afternoon I made a cage for chuck but he got out of the wall. Went after the papers."

May 21: "Went and got the papers, took Barbara with us. (Sis and her came up Friday.)"

May 23: "a fellow came and charged 12 cents to see an oriental war club, an ancient long sword and a short one, a Hindu face ball, a luck charm, an Indian marriage comb and a lot of other things."

May 24: "Ball game. I came home early."

May 25: "School. Same as usual."

May 26: "Ball game. FA vs L.G. Score F.A. 21, L.G. 10. I staid (stayed)."

May 27: "Plowed up on the side hill. Jim got a chuck in the wall. I dug him out after dinner, poked him into a milk can and dumped him into my chuck cage. Mike, Wade, Helen, Bill and Eleanor came down."

May 28: "Made some ice cream. Wade, Helen, Bill and Eleanor went up to M.C.'s." (Note: Wade and Helen are Robert's brother and sister-in-law.)

May 29: "Finished plowing up on the hill. Went down and cut six trees for my log cabin. I came up and went to the village, got a box of strawberries. I got 'The River's Edge' by James Oliver Curtwood and Mother got two pairs of stockings."

May 30: "Made ice cream."

May 31: "Went to school. Came home early. Ball game. Went down to Goodnow's and got a bed and two chairs, the same which Sis sent up from the city by him. Got Ma a dish."

June 1: "Went to school. Came home and found Wade had been here and gave Mother four lobsters. I'm saving some of the shells."

June 2: "Went to school, let out at the end of the 6th period. Basketball game. I came home early."

June 3: "Rainy day. Fixed horse stalls."

June 4: "Picked rocks found a skunk's den. Jim (the dog) killed one baby and I got four alive. Put them (baby skunks) on Pieface (a female pig) and I guess she will take care of them."

June 5: "Mother's birthday. She got 2 dishes, an apron and 4 post cards. My skunks are coming fine. Went to school."

June 6: "Went to school. Skunks got their eyes open."

June 7: "School. Leavitt trimed Mc Falls 15-3."

June 8: "Tried to operate on a skunk and I made a mess of it. I guess I didn't hurt him much though. I didn't get his smell gun nughter (Neutered?). He is alright now."

June 9: "School. Got out at 2 o'clock and sold three tickets to the commencement concert."

June 10: "Rainy day. I sheered two sheep, cut off one sheep's tail, and disarmed two skunks."

June 11: "I Disarmed another skunk. Skunks getting along fine. Went and got the Sunday papers.

June 12: "Got some grain and a bushel of silage seed. It is most cold enough to have a frost. School."

June 13: "Last day of regular school this term."

June 14: "Took exam in chemistry. Got home at noon and harrowed in the afternoon."

June 15: "Didn't do much of anything in forenoon, went and passed in agri and took English test at LG in afternoon."

June 16: "Cultivated and hoed and harrowed."

June 17: "Planted corn in forenoon. Did nothing but read in forenoon. Rainy."

June 18: "Rainy. Nothing doing."

June 19: "Sawed wood. Still rainy."

June 20: "Got washing water. Rained. Went to concert in the evening."

June 21: "Went to graduation. I am now a senior. Got 84 in civics, 70 in chemistry. 73 in English and 75 in agriculture."

June 22: "Sawed wood. Rainy."

June 23: "Still rainy. Sawed wood. Went down and knocked the bottom out of the boat."

June 24: "Sawed wood in forenoon. I am going to put one bottom in the boat, get a strip of tar paper tonight when I go to the movies and put it on it and nail another bottom over that. I guess it'll be tight. It's done."

June 25: "Worked on the boat."

June 26: "Got some more tar paper and finished the boat and put it in the water, and it don't leak very bad."

June 27: "Sawed wood."

June 28: "Went to the circus. Saw trained lions, tigers, leopards, polar bears, seals, pigeons, dogs, horses, and bears. There were giraffes, zebras, camels, dromedaries, panthers, antelopes, elephants, kangaroos, etc. in the animal tent."

June 29: "Pa went to the city. Bradford came along."

June 30: "Cultivated."

July 1: "Worked, went to movies and shingled."

July 2: "B.J. up here. (Bradford Johnson)"

July 3: "Dorrie came up with Barbara B."

July 4: "Made ice cream. B.J. up here"

July 7: "Worked on my log cabin."

July 10: "Worked on my cabin."

July 14: "Kind of under the weather. Didn't do much but start a ceiling in my log cabin."

July 17: "Hoed corn for five hours in the forenoon and worked on my log cabin in the afternoon with BJ's help. BJ is Dad's best friend Bradford." Or (BJ…)

July 21: "Worked haying and started my chimney on log cabin. Earned $2.75, $1.00, .75 cents, and $3.00 from Frank Bray in July."

July 22: "Worked on my cabin and hayed for Frank Bray."

July 23: "Made a door for my log cabin and put it on."

July 24: "Poisoned potatoe bugs. Worked on my cabin."

July 26: Worked haying for Frank Bray. Caught a skunk over there and I carried him home in a nail keg. I got him in my rabbit house now. He's a full grown, narrow-striped specimen of the North Americanus skunk.

July 27: "Cloudy. I picked up shingles after I got home from the village. After dinner I worked on a pen for the skunk till Pop called me to cultivate. After that Mother and I went to the village again, after which I ate supper, milked, and worked on my skunk pen till near dark."

July 28: "Went to the village with the milk. Carried Frank's skunk trap so's I can come to some sort of agreement with as to the ring I busted on it. I took over one of mine but he wasn't home so I left them there. Hope to go there haying this afternoon. I got home, put out the sheep, fed my skunks and Pop and I cultivated the garden above the house. I got the fountain pen in the mail that I have been looking for a week."

July 29: "Worked for George Mitchell. After I got through at about 5:45 I went over to Frank's and got a dead hen for my skunk and a $10.00 spot which he owed me for haying. Next, I stopped over at Allie's and got a black hound pup. I told him I could let him have $3.00 on him but he couldn't change my 10 bucks so I went over to Stop's and got it busted. I let Edgar hold the pup while I went back over to Allie's and paid him. Went back to Earl's, mounted my cayuse and started home. Mother met me half way down the hill and that night when we went to the pictures I carried Sir Pup back and reclaimed my $3:00. The young skunks which I put out in the morning got out, Mother caught 2 of them."

July 30: "Got up at 8:30 and started my skunk pen, then I helped Pop furrow out for some corn. Aunt Josie came up. I finished my pen and put the skunks in it a'fore dinner. After dinner I went down to Johnson's an' got the papers which he brought in the village. Bradford came up with me. We watched the big and little skunks get acquainted awhile an' then went down an' looked at the camp and drove the cows up as we came back. I milked, fed the horse and mowed some ——? to help Marrion and Catherine find the other two skunks but we didn't have any luck. Mother and I carried Aunt Josie home and came home through the potatoe road."

Becky at the back door leading into the kitchen.

Dorrit Josephine Harris 1896–1989
Robert Beckley Harris 1905–1984
Wade Arman Harris 1891–1972
Fred Wilson Harris 1893–1914

July 31: "Bradford came up and we had ice cream for dinner and worked on the log cabin all afternoon."

Aug. 1: "Finished George Mitchell's haying, hotter than death up in his barn. Sent our order to Russel's."

Aug. 2: "Fooled around the forenoon and went to the city with Mr. Johnson in the coupe. He carried Mrs. Johnson and Mis Bradford to take the train and he invited me to go also. B. and I went to a show. Strand, had some ice cream in the candy kitchen. I bought a lot of candy and brought it home. We drove home around the lake and it was a very pretty ride. We started at 1-30 and got home at 6-15."

Aug. 3: "Got a card from Russell's saying they received our order and would send as soon as possible."

Aug. 3: "Started haying but it rained and B and I walked home an met Mother with Romeo (the horse) so we got in and went back to the village and got some fish scraps for the skunks and some fish."

Aug. 4: "Went haying in the afternoon. In the forenoon I weeded the garden and worked on my cabin. Frank Bray called up and said he had another skunk caught in a trap. I made a box with a door in each end and we went haying. I raked up the hay in Lombard's and went over to Frank's with my skunk box. I tied a string to the trap chain and passed it through to the box and hauled the skunk in.

Aug. 4: I pulled the trap through and slid the door down on his leg so he couldn't get out and put in the other door, after which I took the trap off and carried him up to Durgin's. We got in one load of hay before a deuce of a shower. After the shower we came home and I put my skunk in the pen."

Aug. 5: I shook out the hay. I raked and we got in Durgen's and carried one load home from Lombard's field. Bradford, Mother and I went to the movies and saw "The Sea Wolf" by Jack London. I got a letter from Russel's saying they had sent our order."

Aug. 6: "Went out and got two loads of hay from the field and got home and found Howard and Mrs. Gordon an' Wade and Helen and the kids here. They didn't stay long. Mother and I went riding in the afternoon. I finished the roof of the cabin."

Aug. 7: "Kind of rainy. Bradford and I went to the village with the milk and we got our stuff from Russell's. Everything is satisfactory. The hunting knives are great. Mother and I sent "The Lure of the Border" to Harry Carey. Bradford broke the point of his knife but I ground it down again so it's alright."

Aug. 8: "Finished the hay fork track, mowed, and went to the village."

Aug. 9: "Went with the milk. Got home, poisoned bugs. Mr. Johnson and Rathune came up and he and Bradford came up and he and Bradford and K. and I went down to camp. He said he would stake us to half the boards for our cabin roof and lend us the money for the other half. Pop and I hayed all afternoon."

Aug. 10: "Finished the hay we had cut and got it in the barn. Went out and finished Durgin's haying. Got some fish and the boards for the cabin roof."

Aug. 11: "Cut bushes in the forenoon and worked on my cabin roof in the afternoon. Got mor'n half done."

Note: On August 6, Dad wrote "finished the roof of the cabin". Then August 11 he mentions getting the boards and working on the roof. (My only guess is he was referring to the earlier entry some pre work for putting the boards down.)

Aug. 12: "Went and got some wood for my showshoe frames. Went to the village after the papers, stopped down at Johnson's and played golf with Betty and B. and K, Had some ice cream, got home and had some more."

Aug. 14: "Went with the milk. B and I went down to camp. Made ice cream for dinner. Caught skunks in boxtraps that got out of pen."

Aug. 20: "George Staples came and I showed him my cabin. Mother and I went riding and I made two chairs for camp after I got home."

Aug. 21: Bradford and I added two feet on the chimney, chinked up the front and part of one side and put in most of the floor and got the bed frame ready for the fur boughs on the log cabin. He's going the 20th."

Aug. 22: "We chinked up the most of the rest of it."

Aug. 23: "We carried down our kit, dishes etc., finished chinking up, made another bed and finished the other one, finished the floor. Mr. Johnson, Bradford and I stayed down there all night. Had a great time of it."

Aug. 24: "We made some candy down there at 11 AM and went up to dinner. Bradford stayed all night with me up here. (The cabin is at the base of a hill and the house was on top of the hill, hence we went up to the house or went down to the cabin. The house has since been torn down but the cabin survives.)"

Aug. 25: "William, Alvin, Bradford, and I hauled rocks with Romeo for the chimney. Had dinner and hauled rocks till 2-30 in the afternoon. Mother and I went to the village and got a loaf of bread and the mail."

Aug. 26: "Rainy. Didn't do much of anything."

Aug. 27: Went down to camp. Mother and I went to the village after the papers. Got a "Herald" for Mr. Johnson. While we went over to Green's with the rest of the family, Mr. and Mrs. Johnson, Bill Irish and the rest of his family were down to see the camp. We met Mrs. Johnson on the hill and Bradford and Katherine up further. Bradford had a ———? for the camp which his father gave him.

Aug. 28: "I went to the village in the morning. Got home and dug some spuds, then went down to see Bradford. I stayed to dinner and played poker."

Aug. 29: "Dorrie and B.B. (Barbara Bishop, Dorrie's daughter) came up. I went and got her an' took 2 pictures of the steeplejack (on the church) in the afternoon. Pop and I finished shingling the porch roof in the forenoon."

Aug. 30: "Dorrie went back to the city and left B.B. with us."

Aug. 31: "Didn't do much of anything but help Mother take care of Barbara. I set 7 traps in the wall next to the sweet corn."

Sept. 1: "I had a skunk in the gap of the wall. I put him in the rabbit house, so called, with other part grown ones. My last years' lamb got snarled up and choked it self to death last night. I cut off a hind 1/4 and fed it to the skunks (part of it) and buried the rest under an apple tree. I am going to try to catch some coon with half of it as bait."

Sept. 13: "Dug potatoes."

Fourteen-year old Robert harnesses Romeo the horse up to go to school.

L-R: Alice, Anne, Aunt Goldie, Grandmother Cerethia, Mother Ruby Harris, Father Robert Harris. In front Betty and Becky Harris

One of the owner's brothers was a Catholic priest and an aide to the Pope in the Vatican. He went on a retreat and stayed in the cabin one winter. He made that cross, and it has been hanging there ever since. (Becky Roberts with the cross.)

About the Author

Becky grew up on Mount Desert Island off the coast of Maine. By the time she was born, the *camp* was the extended family gathering place during the summers. After high school, Becky worked one year as a nanny for a wealthy Massachusetts family. Then came marriage and children, and when they flew the nest, she went back to school to become a nurse. That career took her to Indian Health Service and Bush, Alaska, to care for the Yupik Eskimos. From Alaska, she transferred to New Mexico where she lived and worked on the Zuni and Acoma Indian reservations. Eventually, she retired and transcribed this little diary to be given to family and began to consider the possibility that others might be interested in the daily life of a seventeen-year-old boy living on a farm in rural Maine in 1922.